Vaccinations

Dr. Alvin Silverstein,

Virginia Silverstein, and

Laura Silverstein Nunn

My Health

Franklin Watts

A Division of Scholastic Inc.

New York • Toronto • London • Auckland • Sydney

Mexico City • New Delhi • Hong Kong

Danbury, Connecticut

Photographs © 2001: Corbis-Bettmann: 25; Peter Arnold Inc./Argus Fotoarchiv: 21; Photo Researchers, NY: 18, 26, 29 (Biophoto Associates/SS), 12 (Carlyn Iverson), 11 (Nina Lampen), 23 (Andy Levin), 24 (NIBSC/SPL), 17 (Sheila Terry/SPL); PhotoEdit: 13 (Robert Brenner), 10, 32 (Mary Kate Denny), 19 (Tony Freeman), 34 (Mary Steinbacher), 7 (D. Young-Wolff); Stock Boston: 30 (Spencer Grant), 22 (Bill Horsman); Superstock, Inc.: 4, 9, 28; The Image Works/F. Hoffmann: 6; Visuals Unlimited: 8 (D. M. Phillips), 35 (SIU), 27.

Cartoons by Rick Stromoski

Library of Congress Cataloging-in-Publication Data

Silverstein, Alvin.
    Vaccinations / Alvin Silverstein, Virginia Silverstein, and Laura Silverstein Nunn
  p.   cm.—(My Health)
  Includes bibliographical references and index.
  ISBN 0-531-11874-6 (lib. bdg.)   0-531-15564-1(pbk.)
    1. Vaccination — Juvenile literature [1. Vaccination.] I. Silverstein, Virginia B. II. Nunn, Laura Silverstein. III. Title. IV. Series.
RA638 .S57   2002
615'.372--dc21   20010 17765

Contents

Are You Protected?

How do you feel about going to the doctor? If it's just a checkup, it's no big deal. But if it's time for you to get a shot, oh no! Most people don't like getting shots because they know it may hurt. But shots are important—a little pain now will save you from a lot of pain later.

In the United States, all children are required to be **vaccinated** to protect them from getting certain diseases. These diseases are caused by germs that can get into your body and make you very sick. When you are vaccinated against a disease, you probably won't get that disease, even if you are exposed to the germs that cause it.

Did You Know...

Keeping your vaccinations up-to-date can protect you from getting certain diseases, not only as a child, but throughout your whole life as well.

This doctor is giving her patient a vaccination to protect her from getting a disease.

What would happen if people didn't get vaccinated? Would people still be safe? Some people think that getting **vaccines** isn't necessary. Doctors say that this is wrong and very dangerous.

Just what are vaccines and how do they work? Read on to learn about the diseases that vaccines protect us against and why vaccination is so important. Then see what you think.

Vaccines were created to help keep you from getting sick.

Germs That Make You Sick

Vaccines protect you against **germs** that may invade your body and cause trouble. Germs can make you really sick; some can even kill you. What are germs, and how can they hurt you?

Germs are very tiny creatures that can sneak into your body without your even noticing them. In fact, you need a microscope to see them. Many of them cannot live on their own. These germs can live only inside a *host*—a living animal or plant that provides food and shelter for another organism.

When germs make a home in your body, you get sick.

When germs get inside your body, they can cause some real trouble. Germs don't really mean to cause harm. They are just looking for a cozy new home in which they can get free food and shelter. The nourishment they get from their host gives them the energy they need to survive and reproduce.

There are two main kinds of germs that cause diseases: **bacteria** and **viruses**.

Bacteria get the nourishment they need from the environment in which they live. Many of them live in soil or water. But sometimes, their environment may be inside a person's body. When bacteria get inside your body, they can multiply quickly. One bacterium divides into two bacteria every 20 to 30 minutes. Each one of those quickly grows until it is ready to divide. After a few hours, you could have millions of bacteria in your body! Bacteria give off poisons that can damage or kill body cells. When enough cells are harmed, you feel sick.

Unlike bacteria, all viruses need a host to survive. They depend on the host to live, grow, and reproduce. Viruses don't give off poisons but they can kill cells when they multiply. Each virus invades a body cell and turns the cell into a virus-making factory. When the cell is full of viruses, it bursts open and hundreds of new viruses spill out. Each new virus

This is what a virus looks like under a powerful microscope.

8

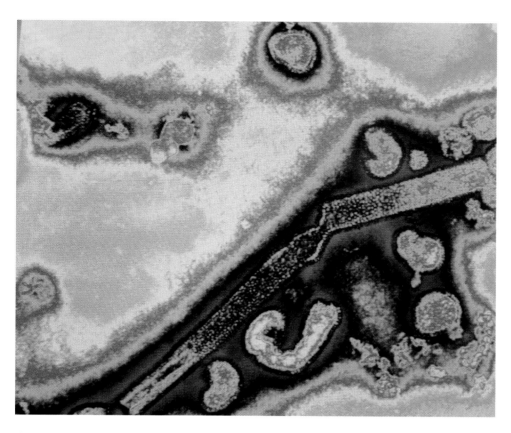

finds a cell to invade and continues the process. Soon there are millions of viruses in your body. As the viruses multiply and spread, you feel sick.

Diseases caused by germs are called **infectious diseases**, and doctors say you are **infected** when germs invade your body and start living and multiplying there. Some infectious diseases are **contagious**—easily passed on from one person to another. Cold viruses, for example, can get into your body when you breathe in tiny droplets of moisture that people with colds sneeze or cough out. Cold viruses may also sneak in if you touch something that some-

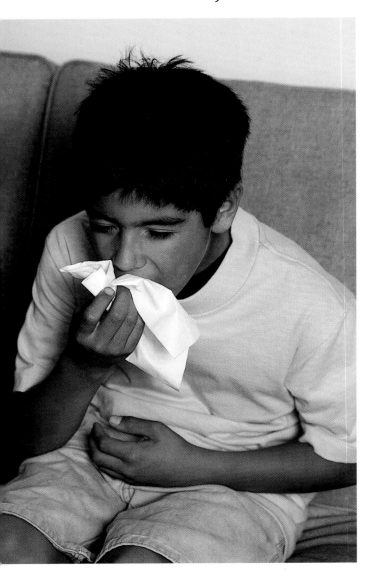

body with a cold coughed on and then put your fingers to your nose, mouth, or eyes. In the warm, moist lining of the nose and throat, the viruses start to multiply.

Germs, such as bacteria, can also be picked up from the environment. For instance, bacteria that live in dirt can get into your body through an open wound. Swimming in water that contains harmful bacteria may allow the bacteria to get into your body through your nose, mouth, or even ears. Germs may also get into your body by hitching a ride on foods that you eat and water you drink. If they multiply inside you, they can make you sick.

Coughing or sneezing into a tissue helps stop the spread of germs.

Your Body's Defenses

When bacteria and viruses get inside you, your body fights back. Some of the germs that enter your nose get trapped in bristly hairs inside your nostrils. Germs that sneak past these hairs fall into a gooey fluid that covers the lining of your nose. This fluid is called **mucus**. Mucus carries the trapped germs to the back of your throat. When you swallow, these germs—plus germs that have entered your mouth—travel to your stomach where they are destroyed in a pool of acid.

Other invading germs are destroyed by your **immune system**. When viruses and bacteria get inside your body cells, those infected cells call for help. They can do this by sending out chemicals to warn nearby cells about the foreign invaders. They need help now, and fast! Soon an army of **white blood cells** comes to the rescue. White blood cells are jellylike blobs that can swim freely through the

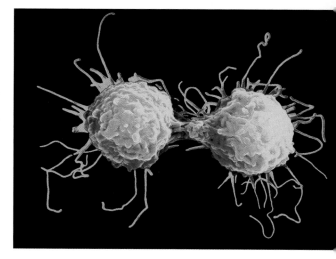

White blood cells help protect your body by attacking germs.

blood. These cells identify invading germs and destroy them. Some white blood cells swarm over the germs and eat them.

Some white blood cells are **killer T cells**. They can detect viruses that are hiding inside body cells. When killer T cells identify an infected cell, they destroy it along with the viruses it contains.

Still other white blood cells, called **B cells**, make special chemicals called **antibodies**. Your body can make thousands of antibodies, each with a slightly different shape. When a disease germ invades your body, cells of the immune system check out the chemicals (called **antigens**) on its outer surface. Then they look for antibodies that match some of these antigens. As soon as a good match is found, the B cells start making more of that particular kind of antibody.

Antibodies fit into a virus or bacterium just as a key fits into a lock. They grab hold of the germ and stick to it tightly. Antibodies may kill germs themselves, or they may make it easier for your white blood cells to destroy them.

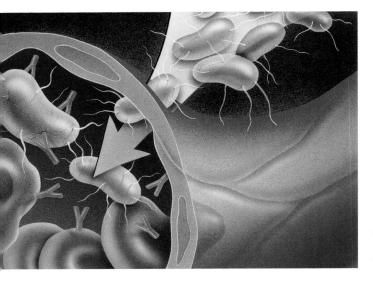

Once the body has made antibodies against a specific disease germ, it keeps some copies even when the illness is over. Then, if the same kind of germ invades your body again, the immune system can quickly make a whole new batch of antibodies to fight the invaders.

That's why you can get chickenpox or measles only once in your life. If the germs that cause these diseases enter your body a second time, your antibodies destroy them right away, before they have a chance to make you sick. Doctors say that you are now **immune** to the disease—you can't catch it again.

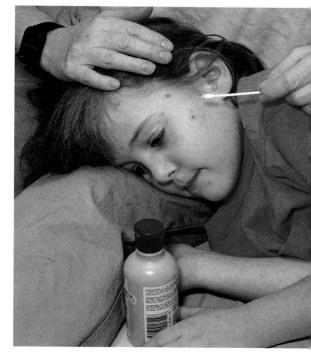

Once you have chickenpox, your body becomes immune to the germs that cause chickenpox.

Got a Cold Again?

More than 200 different kinds of viruses can cause colds. That's why you can get several colds each year. Each cold you get is caused by a different virus than the last one. The antibodies produced during one cold can protect the body only against that specific cold germ.

Activity 1:
Germ Wars

When disease germs invade your body, a fierce battle begins. The germs quickly multiply, trying to outnumber the body's defenders. Your white blood cell "soldiers" come rushing to the scene. Some identify the germs' antigens and others produce antibodies to match them. Here's a game you can play to get the idea of the battle between germs and antibodies. To make it, you'll need some sheets of cardboard or posterboard, scissors, a ruler, a pencil, and crayons or paints.

Rule off a sheet of posterboard into nine equal-size boxes (three rows of three boxes). In the center of each box draw a blue square about 2 inches (5 centimeters) on each side. Divide another sheet of posterboard into nine boxes and draw a 2-inch yellow circle in the center of each box. Do the same with another sheet, but put a 2-inch red triangle in the center of each box. Cut along the dividing lines of each sheet to make a deck of 27 playing cards. These are the antibodies. On another sheet of posterboard, draw six 2-inch blue squares, six 2-inch yellow circles, and six 2-inch red triangles and carefully cut them out. These are the antigens.

This game is for up to three players. If you want to have more, make additional cards and antigens with different shapes—such as a green rectangle or a pink heart. To start the game, each player picks a shape and gets all six antigens of that kind. Then the antibody cards are shuffled and each player receives three cards. If any cards match that player's antigens, the card is placed face-up on the table, and an antigen shape is laid on top of it. If the player has one or more matches, he or she picks enough cards to bring the hand back to three.

If none of the antibody cards has the right shape to match the antigens, the player's picks another card from the deck. (That is similar to the way the body's defenses check for the right kind of antibodies to match the antigens on an invading germ.) The player places a card on the discard pile and then the next player takes a turn. The player who finds cards that match all six antigens is the winner.

How Do Vaccines Work?

The first effective vaccines were created more than 200 years ago. Before that time, millions of people died from diseases to which they were exposed. Smallpox, for instance, used to be a common childhood illness. It was also one of the world's deadliest diseases. Smallpox killed millions of people and left millions more with scars.

The First Effective Vaccine

Dr. Edward Jenner

In 1796 an English doctor named Edward Jenner made the first recorded vaccination. Dr. Jenner found that he could protect people against smallpox by injecting them with liquid, pus, or scabs from the sores of patients with cowpox. This is a much milder disease that is caused by a virus related to the smallpox virus. Dr. Jenner first gave this cowpox vaccine to an eight-year-old boy. A week later, the boy developed mild symptoms: headache, chills, and loss of appetite. Seven weeks after the boy's vaccination, Dr. Jenner injected him again, but this time with smallpox material. The boy did not get smallpox—the vaccine had worked!

The term "vaccination" comes from the medical name for cowpox, *vaccinia*, which comes from the Latin word for cow, *vacca*. Dr. Jenner's smallpox vaccine worked because the antigens on the cowpox (vaccinia) virus are very similar to those on the smallpox virus, so they both fit the same antibodies. Nobody knew that back in 1796, though. In fact, scientists didn't discover that germs cause infectious diseases until more than 80 years later.

How do vaccines work? Vaccines contain substances that stimulate the body to produce antibodies against the germs that cause infectious diseases. These antibodies protect a person from becoming infected even if he or she is exposed to a disease-causing germ. Vaccination is sometimes called immunization because a vaccine produces immunity.

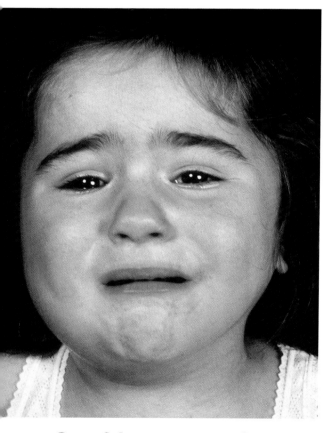

One of the symptoms of measles is a rash. This child has the rash on her face.

Most vaccines are made from the germs they are supposed to protect against. Some contain bacteria or viruses that are alive, but weakened. These are called live vaccines. These weakened germs are changed so that they cannot reproduce and cause a particular disease. However, using these vaccines does involve a small risk of causing the disease if something changes the germs to an active form. Examples of live vaccines are the measles, mumps, and rubella vaccines.

Other vaccines contain disease-causing germs that have been killed, but can still cause the body to produce antibodies. **Killed vaccines** are

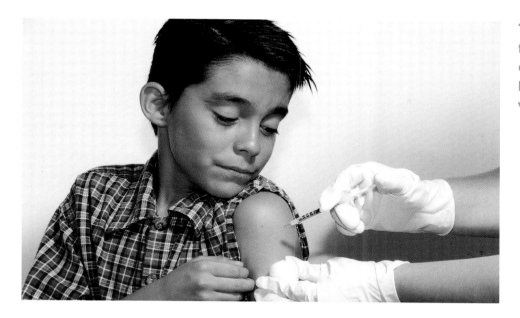

The vaccine for whooping cough is a killed vaccine.

much safer than those that contain live germs. Examples of killed vaccines are those for **rabies** and whooping cough.

Still another kind of vaccine is made to fight the poisons, or **toxins**, that germs produce. These vaccines contain chemically changed forms of the toxins, called **toxoids**. Some examples are the diphtheria and tetanus vaccines.

Recently scientists have been developing new vaccines that contain only parts of germs—antigens—that stimulate the immune system but cannot cause disease. The antigens may also be attached to the vaccinia virus, which helps to stimulate the formation of protective antibodies. (Remember, vaccinia is the virus that was used to make the first vaccine against smallpox.)

Most vaccines are injected into the body. A few, like the live form of the polio vaccine, can be taken by mouth in a squirt of liquid or soaked into a sugar cube. A new flu vaccine can be sprayed into the nose.

With some vaccines, just one dose gives lifelong protection against a disease. For others, it may take several doses to provide immunity. For some, more doses need to be given every five or ten years to maintain the body's defenses. These extra doses are called **booster shots**. Booster shots help to make the vaccine more effective and last longer.

Temporary Protection

Most vaccines produce immunity about two weeks after they are given. Some vaccines, however, work almost immediately, but the protection they give is only temporary. This kind of vaccine is made from **serum** (the liquid part of blood). It contains antibodies that have been produced by another person or an animal. The serum is used to protect people who have been exposed to such diseases as hepatitis, measles, rabies, or tetanus. The protection lasts for only a few months because the antibodies gradually disappear.

Which Vaccines Do You Need?

By the time you were two years old, you probably had been given most of your shots. Vaccinations are so important that health experts recommend vaccinating all children against preventable diseases. That way everyone can be protected from getting these diseases or spreading them to others.

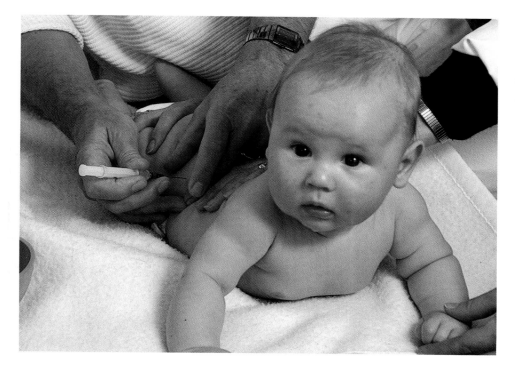

Most vaccinations are given before the age of two.

Protected at Birth

Babies get antibodies from their mothers before they are born. So they start out with protection against all the diseases to which the mother is immune. But most of these antibodies last for only a few months. To stay protected, babies need to develop their own antibodies against disease germs. Vaccination can help them do this without them actually getting the diseases.

Vaccinations can keep even unborn babies safe.

Which diseases do vaccines prevent? In the United States, medical experts recommend vaccination against the following diseases: diphtheria, tetanus, pertussis, polio, measles, mumps, rubella, hepatitis B, varicella (chickenpox), bacterial pneumonia, and **Haemophilus influenzae type b** (or **Hib**). Except for tetanus, all of these diseases are contagious and can be spread from one person to another.

Diphtheria. This is a serious disease that is caused by the poisons produced by bacteria. The illness usually starts out in the throat and can cause swallowing or breathing problems. It may also lead to other serious problems such as **paralysis** (an inability to move) or heart problems. Diphtheria used to be very common. In 1921, more than 200,000 cases and more than 15,000 deaths were reported.

Tetanus. You can get tetanus if you step on a dirty, rusty nail that is carrying tetanus bacteria. Tetanus bacteria, which are found in soil and dust, multiply quickly when they get into deep wounds. If these bacteria spread into your bloodstream, their poisons can cause a condition called **lockjaw**. Your jaw muscles get so stiff that you can't move them to eat or talk. Tetanus

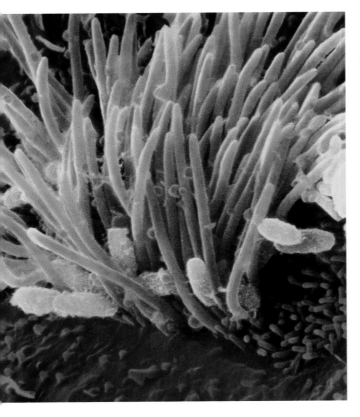

bacteria can even cause death. The tetanus vaccine does not give you lifelong protection. You should get a booster shot every ten years to stay protected.

Pertussis. This bacterial disease is also known as whooping cough. It causes severe coughing spells, which can interfere with eating, drinking, and breathing. Whooping cough is most serious in young children, and many of them need to go to the hospital. Before the vaccine was available,

This is a microscopic view of the whooping cough bacteria.

there were as many as 260,000 cases of the disease each year, with up to 9,000 deaths. In recent years, there have been about 2,000 cases of whooping cough every year, and an average of nine deaths. Doctors say these numbers could be much lower, but only 39 of the 50 states require children to be vaccinated against pertussis.

Doctors routinely combine diphtheria, tetanus, and pertussis vaccines in a single shot called the **DTaP** vaccine.

Polio. This disease is caused by a virus. A mild case of polio may produce symptoms such as fever, sore throat, nausea, headache, and stomachache. In some cases, the person may feel pain and stiffness in the neck, back, and legs. More severe cases of polio may damage nerves that move muscles and can lead to paralysis. In 1952, more than 50,000 polio cases were reported. Compare that to the eight to ten cases caused by the polio vaccine that are reported each year in the United States today.

Franklin D. Roosevelt, the thirty-second President of the United States, suffered from polio.

Measles. This viral disease usually produces symptoms such as rash, high fever, cough, runny nose, and watery eyes. But sometimes, measles may become more serious and possibly life-threatening. For instance, it can lead to a dangerous condition called **encephalitis** (swelling of the brain).

The Reappearing Act

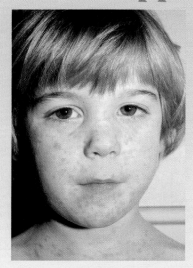

People need to have the measles vaccination twice.

In 1964, there were 484,000 measles cases reported in the United States and more than 400 deaths. After the measles vaccine became available, reports of new cases dropped dramatically. By 1984, fewer than 1,500 measles cases were reported in the United States. But in 1989, thousands of new measles cases suddenly reappeared.

What happened? The new measles cases seemed to be affecting two main groups of people: 1) young, poor children who had never been vaccinated, and 2) college students who had been vaccinated as infants. Health officials realized that a single dose of measles vaccine was not enough to give life-long protection. So recommendations for measles vaccination were changed to two doses of the vaccine. By the mid-1990s, the number of measles cases had once again dropped dramatically. But vaccination must be continued to keep the disease from coming back.

Mumps. This viral disease usually produces a fever, headache, and swollen cheeks. In some cases, the disease leads to serious problems, such as **meningitis** (swelling of the coverings of the brain) and more rarely, encephalitis (swelling of the brain itself).

Rubella. This viral disease is also called German measles. It is usually mild, causing a slight fever and a rash that appears on the face and neck, and it lasts for a few days. Rubella can be a serious problem for pregnant women, however. A woman who gets rubella early in her pregnancy has a chance of giving birth to a baby with birth defects.

Doctors routinely combine the measles, mumps, and rubella vaccines in a single shot called the **MMR** vaccine.

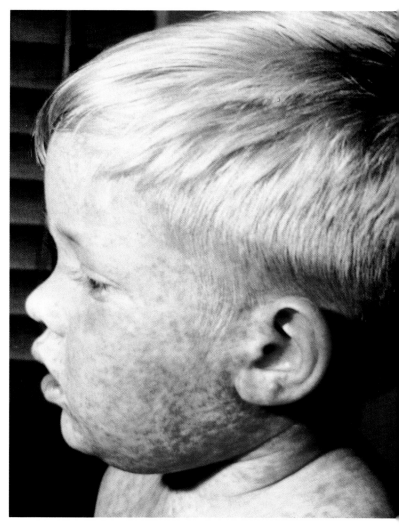

German measles, or rubella, causes a fever and a rash on the face and neck.

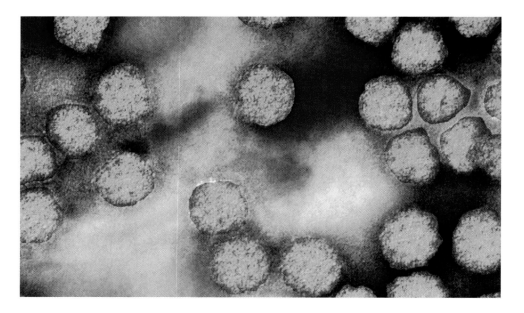

Hepatitis B. The virus that causes this disease can be spread from one person to another through blood, body fluids, or breast milk. Even a pregnant women with the virus can pass it on to her baby during birth. Some people who have hepatitis B carry the virus for their whole lives. Some people may develop serious complications such as liver problems, while other people may not have any symptoms. Unfortunately, these people can spread the disease and not even know it.

Chickenpox. In 2001 the chickenpox vaccine, Varivax, was added to the list of recommended vaccines. Chickenpox is a highly contagious viral disease that causes a fever and an itchy rash to appear all over the body. It is usually considered a mild illness, but sometimes it can become much more serious. It causes a hundred deaths each year.

Haemophilus influenzae type b (Hib). Hib is the name of a bacterium that can cause very dangerous illnesses. Until the vaccine became available, it was the most common cause of meningitis in babies and young children. The 20,000 cases caused by Hib each year also included pneumonia (a lung infection) and serious infections of the heart, blood, bones, and joints. Hib meningitis used to kill 600 children each year. Now there are fewer than ten deaths each year.

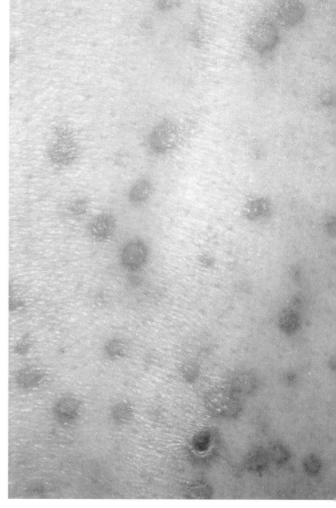

The chickenpox virus causes an itchy rash to appear all over the body.

Influenza. Some people get a flu shot to protect them against the flu every year. The flu (short for influenza) is a very contagious illness that produces a lot of miserable symptoms, including high fever, chills, headaches, achy muscles, cough, and sore throat. Flu

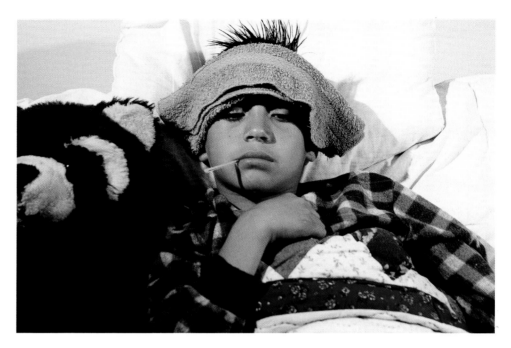

can be very serious for some people because it can lead to other serious illnesses, such as **bronchitis** (swelling of the air tubes leading into the lungs) or **pneumonia**, caused by bacterial infections. Pneumonia is a very serious condition in which the tissues in the lungs swell and the tiny air spaces fill up with fluid. Breathing becomes very difficult, and some patients die.

People need to get a new flu shot each year because the vaccine protects against only the kinds of flu viruses that are around at the time. Year to year, the flu viruses change and a new vaccine is needed.

Recommended Immunization Schedule

Birth to 2 months	Hepatitis B (Hep B)
1 to 6 months	Hep B
2 months	DTaP, Hib, Polio, PCV (pneumococcal conjugate)
4 months	DTaP, Hib, Polio, PCV
6 months	DTaP, Hib, PCV
6 to 18 months	Hep B, Polio
12 to 15 months	Hib, MMR, PCV
12 to 18months	DTaP, Chickenpox (VZV)
4 to 6 years	DTaP, MMR, Polio
11 to 12 years	Tetanus, Diphtheria (Td). This shot should be continued every ten years thereafter.)

Are Vaccines Safe?

Yes, vaccines are safe, but sometimes they can cause reactions. Usually the problems are mild, such as a redness or soreness where the shot was given. Serious reactions are very rare. The fact is, it is more dangerous to get the actual disease than it is to get a shot that can prevent it.

Vaccines You Can Eat

Many children don't like shots. But this may not be a problem sometime in the future. Researchers have been working on vaccines that you can eat. They are growing special plants that contain antigens from disease germs. Eating a banana, tomato, or lettuce with these antigens can make the body form protective antibodies without any danger of causing illness. Edible vaccines will be easier to take than shots—and they won't give you a sore arm!

Someday we may be able to get a vaccine by eating a banana.

Until recently, most polio doses had been given orally (by mouth) in a liquid. Polio vaccines come in two forms: the oral one, which contains live but weakened germs, and the injectable, killed polio vaccine, which contains killed germs.

Doctors like giving the oral polio vaccine for two main reasons: 1) it's easier to give to children, and 2) it gives long-lasting protection. The weakened virus passes into the saliva and stool for a few weeks after the vaccination. It may then be spread to unvaccinated people, which gives them immunity as well, just as if they had been vaccinated. In most people, the vaccine produces very mild symptoms or no symptoms at all. Sometimes, in a small number of cases, the vaccine virus changes and has the ability to produce paralysis. This small risk has caused a great deal of concern for parents.

Recently, U.S. health officials decided to eliminate the risk of the oral polio vaccine and no longer recommend giving it to children. Doctors must now give children four doses of injectable killed polio vaccine, which cannot cause the actual disease.

Did You Know…

Until 1999, the eight to ten polio cases that occurred in the United States every year were caused by the vaccine itself. But compared to the 20 million doses of polio vaccine given to U.S. children each year, that is a very small number!

Medical experts continue to test vaccines to make sure that they are the safest they can be. When problems occur, researchers work hard to develop better vaccines. For instance, doctors used to give patients a DTP shot, but found that some kids were having bad reactions to the pertussis vaccine. Now doctors use a newer vaccine, called DTaP, which is very effective and produces far fewer reactions than the old one. The "a" stands for *acellular*, which means no cells. The new vaccine does not contain whole pertussis bacteria, but just parts of them.

Even though sometimes shots hurt, it is better than getting really sick.

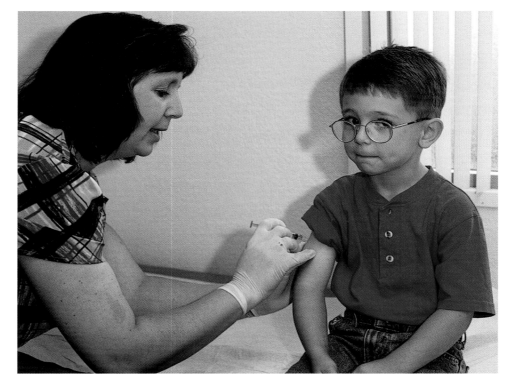

What If We Stopped Vaccinations?

Why should we keep getting vaccinated for diseases that hardly anybody gets anymore? You probably don't know anybody who has had polio or whooping cough. As you now know, before there were vaccines, many children died from these diseases, and those same germs are still around. Fortunately, most kids are protected, so we don't see these diseases making people sick very often.

If we stopped vaccinating people, the children born each year would not have any protection. The germs in the environment would infect them, and preventable diseases would eventually spread throughout the population again.

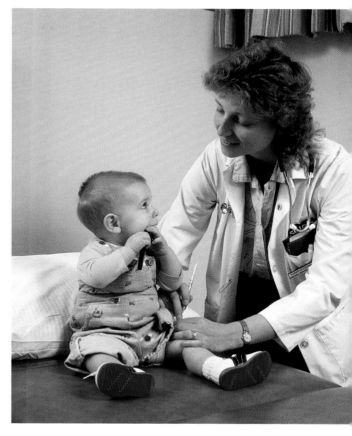

This doctor is giving this toddler a shot in his leg.

As long as there are people in the community who are not protected against diseases, we will need to continue giving vaccines. The more people who are immune to a disease, the less chance that the germ causing it will find an unprotected host and spread to others. This is called **herd immunity**. If the community is protected, then you are too. For instance, if only 50 percent of the population is protected against a particular disease, the germs that cause it have a good chance of finding a suitable host. But if 90 percent or more of the population is protected, the germs are less likely to spread. Eventually, this kind of disease germ will just die out. That's what happened with smallpox.

There is another reason why vaccinations should not be stopped. As long as a particular disease occurs anywhere in the world, a traveler to one of the areas where it is common can pick it up and bring it back home. Then you would be in danger if you were not protected. For instance, polio is very close to **eradication**. It no longer occurs in most of the world, but there are still many polio cases in parts of India and Africa. In order for vaccination to be successful and eventually get rid of some of the world's diseases, we need *everybody's* help.

Activity 2:
Who's Protected?

Use this survey to find out if your friends and family are protected against all the preventable diseases. If you include people of different ages, you will find some big differences. For instance, your grandparents may not have been immunized against polio because the vaccine was not available when they were children. Some of your friends or relatives may have had polio shots or the oral vaccine or both.

Ask each person the following questions and organize your findings in a chart.

1. What year were you born?

Ask questions 2–4 for each of the following diseases: diphtheria, tetanus, pertussis, polio, measles, mumps, rubella, hepatitis B, Haemophilus influenzae type b (Hib), chickenpox, flu, and smallpox.

2. Have you ever had the disease? If so, how old were you?

3. Have you ever been immunized against the disease?

4. If so, how many doses did you receive? At what ages?

5. In the case of polio, what kind of vaccine did you receive?

Glossary

antibodies—special germ-fighting chemicals produced by white blood cells

antigens—chemicals on the outer surface of germs

bacteria—type of germs; single-celled organisms too small to see without a microscope. Some bacteria cause diseases when they get into the body.

B cells—type of white blood cells that produce antibodies to protect against disease germs

bronchitis—swelling of the air tubes leading into the lungs

booster shot—a dose of vaccine given to continue the effect of a previous one

chickenpox—a highly contagious disease that produces a fever and a blistery rash all over the body

contagious—easily spread from one person to another

diphtheria—a disease caused by the poisons of bacteria; the disease starts out in the throat and may cause swallowing and breathing problems.

DTaP—a single shot that combines three vaccines: diphtheria, tetanus, and pertussis

encephalitis—swelling of the brain

eradicate—to remove or destroy completely

germs—tiny creatures such as bacteria and viruses that can cause sickness

Haemophilus influenzae type b (Hib)—a kind of bacterium that can cause very dangerous illnesses, including meningitis and pneumonia

hepatitis B—a viral disease that remains in the blood and can be spread to others through blood, body fluids, or breast milk

herd immunity—protection of all members of a community from a disease as a result of enough of the members having been immunized against it

host—a living plant or animal that provides food and shelter for another creature

immune—protected from a disease

immune system—the body's disease-fighting system, which includes white blood cells

infectious disease—an illness caused by germs

influenza—also known as the flu; a contagious viral disease that produces such symptoms as a high fever, muscle aches and pains, headache, sore throat, and cough

killed vaccine—a vaccine that contains dead germs

killer T cells—type of white blood cells that can detect viruses that are hiding out in body cells

live vaccine—vaccine that contains live, but weakened, germs

lockjaw—condition of being unable to move the jaw muscles

measles—a viral disease that causes small red spots, fever, and coldlike symptoms

meningitis—swelling of the coverings of the brain

MMR—a single shot that combines three vaccines: measles, mumps, and rubella

mucus—a gooey liquid produced by cells in the lining of the nose and breathing passages

mumps—a viral disease that usually produces a fever, headache, and swollen cheeks. In severe cases, it may lead to more serious problems, such as meningitis.

paralysis—inability to move

pertussis—also known as whooping cough. This bacterial

disease causes severe coughing spells, which can interfere with eating, drinking, and breathing.

pneumonia—a very serious lung disease caused by viral or bacterial infection in which the air spaces in the lungs fill up with fluid and breathing becomes difficult. Bacterial pneumonia following flu may result in death.

polio—a very contagious viral disease that, in its severe form, can attack nerves that control the movements of the body, and may lead to paralysis

rabies—a deadly disease caused by a virus that is transmitted by an infected animal

rubella—a viral disease that causes a fever, cough, and a red rash. It is usually mild, but it can cause serious problems in pregnant women, whose unborn children may develop birth defects.

serum—portion of blood that contains antibodies produced by another person or animal; it can provide temporary, but immediate, protection after exposure to a disease germ

tetanus—a dangerous disease caused by bacteria that can grow only where there is no air, such as inside a deep wound

toxins—poisons

toxoids—poisons that are changed chemically to be used in vaccines, such as diphtheria and tetanus vaccines

vaccination—the process of being immunized against a disease or illness

vaccine—a preparation containing an inactivated or weakened virus or bacterium (or portions of it) that is used to stimulate the body's production of antibodies against the germ

viruscthe smallest kind of germ; it cannot even be seen with an ordinary microscope

white blood cells—jellylike blood cells that can move through tissues and are an important part of the body's immune defenses

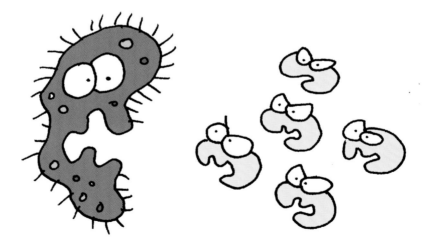

Learning More

Books

Berger, Melvin. *Germs Make Me Sick*. New York: HarperCollins Publishers, 1995.

Griffey, Harriet. *Immunization*. Boston: Element Books, Inc., 2000.

Offit, Paul A. and Louis M. Bell. *Vaccines: What Every Parent Should Know*. New York: IDG Books, 1999.

Shulman, Neil, Todd Stolp, and Robin Voss. *The Germ Patrol: All About Shots for Tots....and Big Kids, Too!* Atlanta: Rx Humor, 1997.

Organizations and Online Sites

The National Immunization Program
Centers for Disease Control and Prevention
1600 Clifton Road, Mailstop E-05
Atlanta, GA 30333
404-639-3311

National Immunization Hotline
800-232-2522

Centers for Disease Control and Prevention—National Immunization Program
http://www.cdc.gov/nip/
This site has many links on vaccines, how they work, and why they are so important.

General Information About Immunization
http://www.cdc.gov/nip/Q&A/genqa/geninf3.htm
This site includes questions and answers about shots.

How Your Immune System Works
http://www.howstuffworks.com/immune-system.htm
This site provides information about the immune system and how it works.

Immunization Action Coalition
1573 Selby Avenue, Suite 234
St. Paul, MN 55104
651-647-9009
http://www.immunize.org
This web site provides immunization resources and articles on vaccine hot topics.

Parent's Guide to Childhood Immunization
http://www.hoptechno.com/book42.htm
This site includes information about immunizations and the diseases they protect against.

Parents of Kids with Infectious Diseases (PKIDS)
http://www.pkids.org

This site provides news, immunization information, and "Ask the Experts" where questions can be asked and answered by e-mail.

Vaccines and Immunization: Everything You Need to Know
http://www.babyzone.com/drnathan/medref/immunizations.htm
This site provides information on immunizations.

Your Child's Immunizations
http://kidshealth.org/parent/general/body/vaccine.html
This site has information about immunizations and the diseases they protect against.

Index

Page numbers in *italics* indicate illustrations.